Old ISLAY

by
Gilbert Carmichael

Passenger Plane at Bridgend, Islay.

Photo, CAMERON, BOWMORE.

A plane at 'The Strand'. This flight would have started at Glasgow Airport at Renfrew with a stop at Campeltown on the way.

© 1998 Gilbert Carmichael
First published in the United Kingdom, 1998,
by Stenlake Publishing
Telephone / Fax: 01290 423114
Reprinted 2006
Printed by St Edmundsbury Press Ltd

ISBN 1 84033 024 4

Carrying Seaweed up the Cliffs at Oa, Islay.

Photo. Archd. Cameron, Bowmore.

In the early 1800s most islands produced kelp from seaweed. In Islay it was not feasible due to the lack of suitable seaweed available for regular harvesting. After a storm, however, seaweed would be washed up on shore. This was gathered and used as fertiliser.

Port Wemyss was built as a fishing village in the early 1830s by Walter Frederick Campbell, but really all that separates it from Portnahaven is a burn! He named the village after his father-in-law, the Earl of Wemyss. The first Campbell to take over after 400 years of MacDonald rule was John Campbell of Cawdor who was granted a Royal Charter of ownership about 1615. His family held ownership for the next century but due to rising debt caused by the outlay on the various estates they owned throughout Scotland, they found it necessary to lease Islay to Daniel Campbell of Shawfield in 1725. He was an MP and, as a result of him voting in favour of the malt tax in 1725, his large mansion house in Glasgow was damaged by a mob. The compensation he subsequently received helped finance his purchase of Islay outright in 1726.

Port Wemyss' neighbouring village, Portnahaven, was the earliest fishing village in Islay, the first houses there dating from the early 1700s. As a church wasn't built in Port Wemyss the villagers had to go to Portnahaven and share the church there. Portnahaven's sheltered bay made it ideal as a fishing centre, but as the waters beyond it are second only in danger to those off the north coast of Scotland, the Orsay lighthouse was built. These days many of the old fisherman's cottages are now holiday homes.

PORTNAHAVEN BAY, ISLAY.

The boats in the bay show how busy this village was at the turn of the century when fishing was still a thriving industry. The catch was mostly cod, ling, haddock, plaice and herring, and the fishermen usually sailed to Ballycastle in Ireland to sell it. Another of the village's one-time industries was salt-making which was important for fish-curing. The Treaty of Union of 1707 prohibited the Scots from importing salt from the English and salt-pans for crystallising sea water were set up here and at other locations on the island.

Telephoto View, showing Paps of Jura from West End, Port Charlotte, Islay. 131/209

To accommodate people who were cleared off the lands at Torony, Kilchiaran and Lossit, the construction of Port Charlotte was started in 1823. When Walter Frederick Campbell became Laird in 1816 he realised that to make his land commercially viable there would need to be a major reorganisation of the way it was used and held by the tenants. His answer was to move most of the people into newly built villages and those who were left then had more land to tend and subsequently larger, commercially valuable, crops. As a result he was able to increase the farm rents. As for the new villagers, there were plots of land on which to grow crops and keep a cow, and jobs available as craftsmen, fishermen, weavers or labourers on the larger farms. The wooden building in this picture was used by the auxiliary coastguard for storing life–saving apparatus.

Built of stone from a quarry which was once in the centre of the village, Port Charlotte was by 1829 self-sufficient with a blacksmith, shoemaker, several joiners, three hotels, a school, a church and a thriving distillery. Today many of the houses are holiday homes though two hotels and the school survive. The present church is situated halfway between Port Charlotte and Bruichladdich. The island's creamery is also at the village.

School Street, Port Charlotte, Islay   131/10

The village school was built in 1830 and remained in use until 1976 when a replacement was built on the site of the old village hall. The old school then became the new village hall. In the early days of education on the island, schools were initially under the patronage of the Laird, though the various single teacher schools that were also established were paid for by the parents of the pupils. In 1872 the state took responsibility for all of Islay's schools. The education given in those days was of a high standard and many pupils went on to become ship's captains, doctors and ministers. By the 1950s most of the single teacher schools had been closed and Port Charlotte became the main centre of education for that part of the island.

The main fuel on the island was peat and the prevalent method of transport, at least until the late 1940s, was the horse and cart. It was normal for neighbours to share the task of peat cutting. A visit to the peat moss also gave the opportunity to bring back a large bunch of heather and, tied to a rope, this made an effective chimney cleaner. The men in this picture are Malcolm McLellan (left) and Neil Brown of Shore Street (right).

Port Charlotte's present pier was built in the 1950s. Before that there had been several rubble piers but these were destroyed by winter gales. For a time the best way to get to Bowmore was by ferry but this service ceased in the late 1920s due to an improvement of the standard of roads and the subsequent increase of cars and buses.

The chimney belongs to the village's distillery which was built in 1829. At the height of its production in the late 1880s it was producing 130,000 gallons of whisky a year. The distillery closed in 1929 and the double storey warehouse is now the Youth Hostel. The technique of whisky distilling probably came to Scotland around the fifteenth century and eventually each area of Islay had several small stills producing whisky for instant consumption. The Act of Union in 1707 created the excise board which taxed alcohol production, but by some oversight Islay was omitted from the board's area of control for about 90 years. Thus, it was up to the Laird to collect the tax and as a result illicit stills sprung up all over the island to avoid paying him.

A boat in the bay at Port Charlotte, probably unloading coal for the distillery. When ready for shipment, Port Charlotte's whisky would normally be transported by cart to the pier at Bruichladdich as the village's own pier was still too flimsy to take the boat. However, if the weather was favourable the casks were sometimes taken out on rafts to a boat, like this one, moored in the bay.

Stacking the peats at Coultorsay Farm by Bruichladdich. Peat was cut in the early summer months and enough was collected to last a whole year. The whole operation was very laborious and depended on there being at least three or four weeks of dry weather. Once cut each block had to be laid out singly in the open air for up to ten days so that it would dry for storage. It could then be stacked and the dried peat would be more or less impervious to dampness and rain.

Bruichladdich Distillery.

In 1823 the Excise Act was passed which made conditions much more favourable for whisky distillers. Excise duties were halved and there was even a rebate offered on exports. To qualify for these conditions the minimum size of a still was only 40 gallons. As a result it was suddenly viable for many of the illegal stills to become legitimate and many of the crofters who operated them amalgamated them into larger concerns. Bruichladdich's distillery (which did not originate in this way) was built for the village in 1881 and the buildings were erected in a square and constructed in such a manner that, in the event of a fire, all the buildings would not be destroyed. The business was able to make use of the pier which was built for the village three years earlier for the cargo steamers from Glasgow and for the irregular service to and from Northern Ireland. Weather permitting, the cargo boat, with passenger accommodation, made two trips a week from Glasgow to Islay via Greenock. Until the advent of roll-on/roll-off ferries that could carry freight lorries, the boat had to make the laborious journey around the Mull of Kintyre, a route still in use as late as 1970.

Like every other village on the island, Bruichladdich was a working community and those who were not employed in the distillery worked on the land. The Laird's reorganisations of the 1820s improved agriculture on the island considerably. He introduced the cultivation of flax and the spinning and weaving of linen. Wheat, barley, oats and potatoes were grown, and because they had more land, tenants were encouraged to rotate crops and to leave some ground fallow each year. In the good times the surplus crops were exported and soon the main income for farmers came from the export of cattle to the mainland markets and horses and pigs to Ireland.

Conisby, Islay, showing Lochindaal

There is a legend that a widowed lady with a large family once landed in Islay. She had no money and relied on the islanders to give her food and shelter. At Conisby, just north of Bruichladdich, she was made very welcome and stayed for four weeks. Apparently, when she left she prophesised that the place would become very famous for piping. Is it a coincidence that a lot of pipers came from here in future years?

The parish of Kilchoman consists of the entire Rhinns of Islay. At Kilchoman itself there has been a church since the twelfth century. The present building was built in 1826 and was the parish church until 1935 when St Kieran's at Port Charlotte took over the responsibility. However, the church continued to be used intermittently until 1977 when it was finally closed due its poor state of repair. It is worth visiting the churchyard to see the beautiful Kilchoman Cross. Eight feet, five inches tall, it was carved in one piece. On one side is the figure of Christ surrounded by saints and angels and on the other is a patterned design. Unfortunately, the Latin inscription is now becoming unreadable due to weathering.

Kilnave, Loch Gruinart, Islay.

CLAIDHEAMH O BHLAR TRAIGH GHRUINEARD.
SWORD FROM THE BATTLE OF GRUINART STRAND, 1598.

This sword belonged to an Islayman named McPhee, from whom it was taken when the clansmen were disarmed. McPhee, however, followed the government party from Gruinart to Laggan Strand, where he regained possession of his sword—by what means we know not. On his way he called at Bridgend Inn for a dram "on credit", which the innkeeper refused. McPhee afterwards affirmed that had the dram been given, not a single weapon should have left Islay.

(The sword hilt is one of the famous Islay Hilts, by McEachern, Kilchoman.)

This battle was between the Clan MacLean and the Clan MacDonald who were fighting each other for ownership of the land in the Rhinns. This dispute would rage on until the MacLean's avenged their defeat here by virtually wiping out the MacDonalds at Ben Vicar in 1616, the last battle to take place on Islay. The McEachern's forge was near Kilchoman Church and their swords were much sought after. Typically, there blades were about two inches wide at the hilt and fifty inches long – the swords could be as long as five foot eight inches overall!

ISLAY HOUSE, ISLAY.

Although the construction of Islay House was begun by Sir Hugh Campbell in 1677, the building was still being altered and extended even as late as 1910. This picture shows it before the 1910 extension.

In the early eighteenth century the principal link between Islay and the mainland was the drove road. At that time Islay was exporting around 3,000 cattle annually and an inn was built to accommodate the drovers when they stopped at Port Askaig before ferrying the cattle across to Jura on the way to the Falkirk market. In the 1750s a weekly sailing to West Loch Tarbert was established, carrying the mail and a few passengers.

In 1825 the introduction of the wooden paddle steamer, *Maid of Islay*, allowed an increase to twice weekly of sailings to and from Port Askaig. One sailing was also extended to take in Oban, Mull and Skye, and a weekly sailing between West Loch Tarbert and Port Ellen was also introduced. The boat at the pier is the *SS Hebrides* which earlier this century was a regular caller on the Inner Hebrides run, delivering cargo from Glasgow.

The Steamer entering Portaskaig: Islay.

Photo. Cameron
Bowmore

The *Pioneer* was purpose built for the Islay run and took over from the Glencoe in 1905, sailing from West Loch Tarbert to Port Askaig or Port Ellen alternatively. A lifeboat station was established at Port Askaig in 1934 to deal with the increase of shipping around Islay. The first lifeboat was the *Frederick Pilley* which had been transferred from the Lizard station in Cornwall. This boat was replaced in 1935 by the *Charlotte Elizabeth* which was the first motor lifeboat built in Scotland.

The *Pioneer* was replaced in 1939 by the *Locheil* which operated until the 1960s when the replacement was a car ferry which also carried commercial lorries. Such a replacement was necessary due to the success of Western Ferries who, in 1968, started running a roll-on/roll-off ferry service in competition to MacBrayne's *Locheil*. It was the introduction of these ferries that finally led to the demise of the cargo boats and the puffers.

A photograph of the *Locheil* from the early '60s, (*Locheil* was taken out of service in the late '60s). Alongside are two of MacBrayne's mail buses which took passengers on to Portnahaven and Port Ellen. When the pier was reconstructed the two bollards were discovered to be cannon.

The pier at Port Askaig, taken from the *Locheil* as she departs for West Loch Tarbert.

One of Islay's most remote distilleries is situated at Bunnahabhain at the end of what was once three miles of snaking, single track road. When it was constructed in 1881, houses, a village hall and a school were also built for the workers. In 1823 there were sixteen distilleries on the island but this had dropped to nine by 1887. Nevertheless, this number still consumed more barley than the island could provide. As a result regular deliveries of malt were made once a week by the steamer *Islay*, which also called to take the finished product back to the mainland.

BRIDGEND, ISLAY.

Bridgend is at the central cross-roads of the island where a bridge crosses the River Sorn. It was an ideal stopping point for the cattle on their way to the mainland market and an inn has been here since the early 1700s. The island headquarters of the Royal bank of Scotland were also situated here from 1838 but moved to a new building in Bowmore in 1979.

John McArthur at the reins of his post van. The picture was taken around the turn of the century and at that time McGibbon was the main mail contractor on Islay, supplying the bulk of the transport used for distributing mail.

Driver Neil Gillespie with a later McGibbon vehicle. Such motor buses replaced the earlier horse-drawn vehicles. This Ford, painted Post Office red, was a mail bus and carried passengers as well as the mail.

Aerial View of Bowmore, Islay.
"Bulletin" Copyright Photo

131/197

The village of Bowmore was started in 1768 to replace the village of Killarow which stood adjacent to Islay House. Killarow was a thriving township with its own post office from 1744 and also a church, school, several shops, blacksmith, mill and an inn. The Laird persuaded his tenants there that they should move to Bowmore as the housing conditions would be better and they would have more room to expand their concerns (also it would allow the Laird to have a quieter environment around his house). The focal point of the village is the round church which was constructed by the Laird a year before work on the village began.

Bowmore's pier was constructed in the 1790s, although the local fishermen fished only for local consumption. The main fishing village remained Portnahaven. During the Second World War a seaplane base was established here for the Catalinas and Sunderland Flying Boats that provided anti-submarine cover for convoys sailing to the Clyde ports.

Bowmore from the Pier (Sec. 2)
(Photo. Cameron. Bowmore. Islay)

Apparently, despite being surrounded by water, very few of the locals could swim and it was only through the hard work of the inhabitants that enough money was raised to build an indoor swimming pool. This was constructed in a disused warehouse at the distillery and opened in the early 1990s.

Apart from fishing, weaving and the distillery, another local industry at Bowmore was saltmaking. This was at its height in the late eighteenth century and a reminder of this is Saltpan Point near the town.

BOWMORE DISTILLERY, BOWMORE, ISLAY. *(Estab. 1779.)* | *Head Office :* **7 & 8 Idol Lane, London, E.C.**

Telegram Address : " Distillery." | *Telegram Address :* "*Washback*." | *A.B.C.Code,* *Fifth Edition.*

Bowmore Distillery is the oldest on the island and even today they continue to malt in the traditional way, turning the barley by hand using wooden shovels instead of a mechanised turner. Sometimes during the winter storms sea water has been known to enter the lower warehouses – perhaps this gives the whisky its unique character!

Main Street. Bowmore. Islay.

Photo. Cameron
Bowmore

The Latin inscription above the door of the Round Church reads, 'With pious intent and to promote truth and honour, Daniel Campbell, Lord of this island built, at his own expense in the year of 1767, this church and dedicated it to God'. The design was such that the church had no corners in which the devil could hide.

The building on the right was once used as the island's Sheriff Court but today the nearest court is at Campbeltown and the regional council administers the island from Lochgilphead.

Some natty dressers outside Bowmore's old post office in Shore Street.

The building of Port Ellen commenced in 1821 and like Port Charlotte and Port Wemyss was designed to accommodate the people cleared off the land. A distillery was opened in 1825 and this helped to attract people to the village. It was owned by the Ramsay Family for about 90 years until they sold it in 1920. It closed ten years later but reopened in 1967. It closed for the last time in 1983.

One of Islay's past landowners is remembered by the Ramsay Memorial Hall which was built in Port Ellen in 1902 by Captain Ramsay in memory of his father John who owned the Kildalton estate. He bought the estate from from Walter Frederick Campbell and continued Campbell's policy of clearing the people of the land and encouraging the islanders to move and even emigrate. He cancelled their rent arrears, bought their meagre stock and helped to pay their fares to Canada. He even travelled there in 1870 to visit some of those who had emigrated. For those who stayed, new housing was provided and employment on the construction of the low road between Port Ellen and Bowmore.

PORT ELLEN PIER AND BAY.

NO. 277.

Port Ellen was a principal pick-up point for sheep being transported from this part of the island to mainland markets. Regular weekly sailings from Glasgow to Port Ellen started in 1827 and twenty years later the old wooden pier was rebuilt in stone. This was to accommodate three iron paddle steamers, *Islay I*, *Islay II* and *Islay III*, that served on the Glasgow to Islay run, with occasional calls to Ireland, from 1849 to 1902.

55075.J.V.

The *Pioneer* was specially built for the Islay run in 1905. Her predeccesor, the *Glencoe,* had been in service since 1857 and remained as a standby ship until 1931 when she was eventually sold.

The *Locheil*, pictured in 1960, alongside Port Ellen's then recently rebuilt ticket office and depot. The sling visible on the left was used for lifting cars on and off the ship.

ISLAY SPORTS.

The Islay Sports still continue today and have changed little since this picture was taken around the turn of the century. They continue to be held on what is now Port Ellen's football park and consist of all the favourite events of a Highland Games – piping, highland dancing, hammer throwing, the shot putt, tug of war and races. The building on the right is the White Hart Hotel which is still thriving today.

Lagavilin, Islay

Photo Archd. Cameron

As illicit distilling had been going on there for some time, a legitimate distillery at Lagavulin was built in 1818. In 1908 a small distillery called the Malt Mill was opened adjacent to it and even though it used the same water and peat, the whisky from it tasted entirely different from that of its larger neighbour. The Malt Mill closed in 1962 and was absorbed into the Lagavulin. The company-owned puffer at the pier is the *Pibroch* which was used to transport coal, barley and empty whisky casks. It was replaced in 1953 by a modern diesel puffer, also called the *Pibroch*.

Ardbeg, another distillery, was established in 1815 on a site where whisky had previously been made illegally. The Glasgow steamer called twice a week and if the draff was not wanted by local farmers it would be transported to Larne in Ireland. Draff is the solids left after the barley has been through part of the distillation process. It is rich in protein and makes an excellent cattle feed.

Claggan Bay, Islay.

photo.
Cameron, Bowmore.

At Claggan Bay there was a small sheiling with a boat for fishing and peat for fuel stacked beside the road. The sheiling has disappeared although the road remains a single track.

To encourage his tenants to improve their stock and take pride in their animals, Walter Frederick Campbell established the Islay Show in 1838. It took place on the land just behind Islay House and on display were cattle, sheep, Clydesdale horses and pigs. The show is still going strong today.

Locals pose by a ruined chapel at Kilchiaran on Islay's west coast. It was named after one of St Columba's followers, Ciaran, who landed on the island to build a chapel.